AF481162

I'm always excited whenever my dad and I go downtown to shop at the local stores.

On the way to town, we talked about the needs for the house and our family. My mom always makes us a list before we leave because my dad sometimes forgets a few things.

When we arrive, I can't wait to find the toy store and pick out the latest action figure I want.

I just got my allowance for doing my chores around the house and getting good grades at school. I'm almost a 5th grader.

Before we start shopping, my dad always must have a cup of coffee. He says it makes him happy.

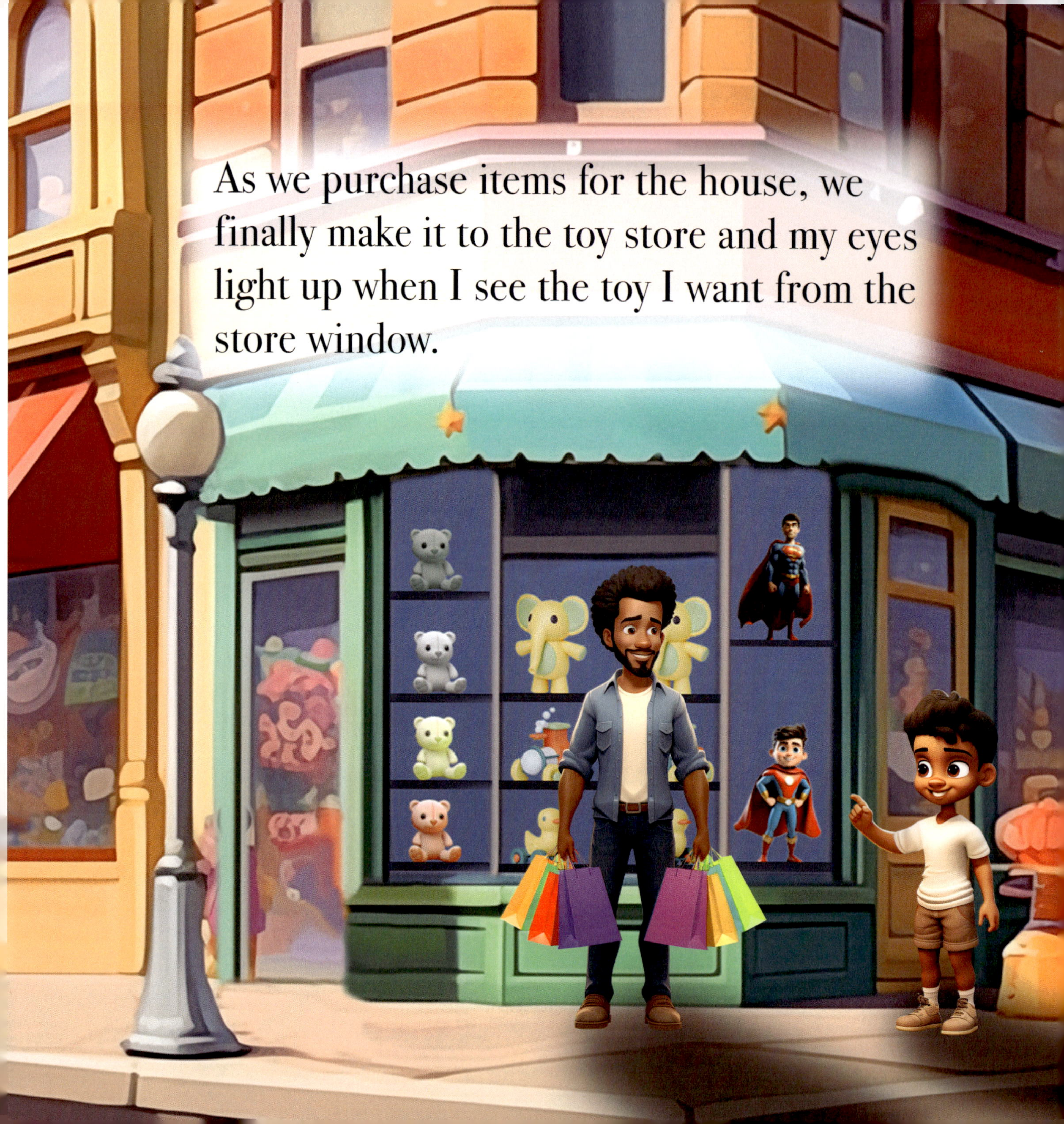

As we purchase items for the house, we finally make it to the toy store and my eyes light up when I see the toy I want from the store window.

When we entered, I noticed there was only 1 action figure left, and I noticed a kid who was looking at the same toy.

He's with his mom and I can hear her say to him, "Son we don't have the money to buy this item right now.

Maybe next time. The boy lowered his head looking very sad and grabbed his mom's hand as they began to walk out of the toy store.

I quickly remembered what my dad said about giving back, helping others, and how important it is to be generous when you can.

My parents always talk to my sister and I about being grateful for the things we have.

I thought about all the toys and games that I had at home. I had a lot to be thankful for. I could take my allowance and buy the toy for myself, or I could use it to help someone else.

I told my dad that I wanted to purchase the toy and give it to the boy who just left the toy store with his mom.

My dad smiled and said are you sure that's what you want to do with your allowance? I said yes.

We purchased the item and quickly caught up to the boy and his mom as they were walking to the bus stop.

We introduced ourselves, my dad and I talked
with the mom about my gesture and wanted to
give her son the toy as a gift of kindness.

The mom was very grateful and happy, and her son was also very excited.

His name is Oliver, and he goes to my school.
He's in the 3rd grade and loves reading comic
books! We talked about possibly hanging out
sometime.

As we drove home my dad asked me how I felt about doing something for other people. I smiled and said I felt good about it.

I told my dad when I got home, I want to go through all my toys and donate the ones I no longer play with to help more kids in our area. Giving back is cool. It makes you feel good, and I can't wait to do more.